SPIRIT REIGN
PUBLISHING
A Division of Spirit Reign Communications

Cover Design: Daryl S. Anderson Sr., Spirit Reign Communications

Page design & layout: OA.Blueprints, LLC

Photographer: Christopher McBrown, Neptune Studios

Food Stylist for photographs: Chef Byron Green

Printed in the United States of America

978-1-940002-79-8 (PB)
978-1-940002-80-4 (ePDF)
978-1-940002-81-1 (ePUB)

SPIRIT REIGN
PUBLISHING
A Division of Spirit Reign Communications

TABLE OF CONTENTS

This book belongs to:

"____"

Preface

The S.N.A.C. it up! cookbook will make children look at eating healthy as the new swag . In this book, 11 year old author, "Shi," engages and inspires even those that do not have a desire to cook. As it is "FOR KIDS BY A KID," it is uniquely written to hold the attention of those with limited attention spans. It contains impressive and delicious recipes like healthy pizza muffins and pomegranate vegetarian chicken. The S.N.A.C. it up! cookbook takes the guess work out of breakfast, lunch, dinner, dessert, and snack! It displays how super easy it is to for a child to be healthy, while creatively educating the reader with fun facts about ingredients after each recipe.

In this cookbook, "Shi" expounds on her famous call and response acronym "S.H.A.R.E.W.I.T.H." to help children remember to include daily aspects of physical and emotional health that are often forgotten or ignored. As she states, "It's about what you eat AND think. " In fact, the book ends with positive thoughts puzzles, as "Shi" recognizes from personal experience that feeling good about oneself brings the confidence needed to make healthy food choices.

This cookbook is not just for "kitchen lovers or "health nuts," it is for EVERYONE that has 2 eyes, a nose, 2 ears, 2 hands, and a mouth! You will catch yourself wanting to pick it up when you are not even close to the kitchen. This cookbook has recipes for the beginner as well as the professional. Wherever you are, you fit!

At 9 years old, "Shi" began working on the cookbook after watching many cooking shows and realizing that with a healthy diet, most of the recipes couldn't be made. She then thought about the fact that this is all that children are exposed to. Oh no! This means that unhealthy eating would become their norm at a very young age. She thought, "hasn't anyone been watching television or billboards to know that childhood obesity and juvenile diabetes are REAL?" Shi then set out to be a solution to the problem. She decided to develop the first S.N.A.C. it up! cookbook and reclaim her peers.

This makes the S.N.A.C. it up cookbook MUCH NEEDED in every child's hand.

Testimonials

"I learned that 'loving myself' is healthy for me. And THE RECIPES in the COOK-BOOK???!!!!! Oooooooh! Everyone MUST get it! I can't stop cooking. I thank God for "Shi."

-Moriah M., 10 years old

"S.N.A.C. It Up! is a great resource for schools because it addresses so many areas of health. Our children ask for her daily, and want to eat right just because "Shi" said it. "Shi" is memorable and timely."

- Yvette Lewis, Director of Title I and II, Utopian for the Arts

Welcome to the S.N.A.C. it up! Cookbook

My name is Shi and I am so excited about all of the recipes in this book. I want you to know how easy and FUN it is to eat healthy. Most of all, IT TASTES sooooo good! I am teaching children how to be healthy so they won't be sick.

Shi

'Shi's Kitchen Commandments"

1. Always ask your mom or dad before you begin to take out ingredients. Ask them to help you with all recipes.

2. If mom or dad says it's ok, wash your hands with soap and water before touching any food.

3. Show mom or dad all of the kitchen tools you will need (ex: knife, fork, spatula). Be VERY careful with sharp objects.

4. Read the recipe completely before getting started. Make sure that you have all ingredients and utensils.

5. Always use potholders or oven mitts to touch hot dishes or pots and pans.

6. Put ingredients away when you are finished with them.

7. Do not put knives or other sharp objects into a full sink.

8. Never run in the kitchen.

9. Always, ALWAYS cook and prepare with love. If you are in a bad mood, think about something positive until you are HAPPY, NOW you are ready to start cooking!

10. Share your food as an act of giving so that someone else can see how easy it is to be healthy.

WHAT DO WE NEED
in order to be healthy?

We need to S.H.A.R.E.W.I.T.H. Share this With everyone that you know.

- **Sunshine**
- Healthy food
- Air
- Rest
- Exercise
- Water
- I love myself
- Trust & Thankfulness
- Help

SUNSHINE

Yeah!!! Who wants to go outside? The sun actually has vitamins. If you spend time outside every day, you can be healthier. Have you ever noticed how happy you are when the sun is shining bright outside? Well, your body on the inside feels brighter when you go outside in the sun. Let's get healthy by smiling back at the sun. You've got to be outside to do that! Come on, let's do it!

HEALTHY FOOD

In order to have healthy food, you must have healthy ingredients. In my family, we try to buy organic fruit and vegetables. If you cannot buy organic, wash your fruit and vegetables very good. You should eat vegetables or fruit with every meal. There are so many different types of vegetables and fruit that you probably have never heard of.

FRESH AIR

Do you smell that? Aaahh. That smells nice. If you can smell the trees, flowers, even the cold air, you MUST be outside. Did you know that we need air to stay alive? When you breathe outside, your body gets oxygen and gets rid of the dirty air in your body. If you want to get rid of the dirty air in your body, you HAVE to go OUTSIDE and breathe. Did you know that children who get lots of fresh air have lower stress, do better in school, and concentrate more?

REST

My brother thought that sleeping was overrated. He liked to sneak and stay up really late, until he started getting sick. My mom and dad found out and told him that our bodies repair themselves at night, but ONLY if you are asleep. So, going to bed early and sleeping ALL night actually helps the body heal and stay healthy. I don't know about you, but I'm going to sleep smiling. I don't like to get sick.

EXERCISE

Being healthy is not healthy without exercise. Get up off of the sofa and wiggle around for 30-60 minutes per day. Our bodies get sluggish if we don't move around. Put the video game down for a while and have fun moving. Your heart, lungs, mind, and more are waiting to be perfectly healthy. They can't do it without exercise. Walking and jumping on the trampoline are my favorite exercises.

WATER

Our bodies are mostly water on the inside. Our bodies get thirsty on the inside and begin to break down when we do not drink enough water. "What about soda?" Oh no! That won't do. Would you put your heart and lungs inside a bowl of soda? "How much water should I drink?" Hmmmm. My mom says that we should drink half of our body weight in water everyday. "Huh?" Ok, if you weigh 60 pounds, then you should drink 30 ounces in water every day. That's about three and a half cups of water per day. Ask your mom how much you weigh and figure out how much you should drink. It will help you be MUCH healthier. Try it and tell me how you feel.

I LOVE MYSELF

It is VERY important to always think good thoughts. We should tell ourselves that we love ourselves at least ten times per day. It is even better to do this with a mirror. Always think that good things can happen to you and other people. Never, NEVER wish any bad on anyone, even if that person does not like you. Smile and say nothing but good things.

TRUST

THANKFULNESS

My mom always tells me that we shouldn't worry about anything. I hear her saying. "Worrying is like carrying heavy bricks for a long time and then you find out that those bricks were not even yours." God is supposed to take care of the bricks, but we take them and weigh ourselves down when we don't have to. Please join me in being happy and light. Also, find an adult that you trust to talk to about the good and the bad things. Never keep secrets that hurt you. Talk to someone quickly because YOU matter.

Always be happy and thankful for even the little things. Instead of complaining about what you don't like, talk about what you do like. It can change everything. Get a journal and start writing down everything that you are thankful for. Write at least two things that you are thankful for every day. Yes, every day. It is fun and it can make you feel better about the bad things that happen. Being healthy is easy when you are thankful.

HELP

My mom and dad always teach my brothers and me to give to someone every day. This means to help someone either by giving kind words, a big smile, or even time to someone that needs help. You can help an older person with their yard or help them clean their house. When I give, lots of good things happen to me. Try it!

Common ingredients used in this cookbook explained:

Note: This cookbook is very friendly to children who have food allergies.

One flax egg: Mix 1 tbsp ground golden flax with 2 tbsp warm water and let sit for 1 minute. Stir with a fork and use. Add water as needed to make it feel like egg.

Egg replacer: This is mostly used for baking. Follow the directions on the box.

Expeller pressed oil: Oil that is from nuts, seeds, grain, and other all natural sources by pressing. These oils are good for your heart, arteries and many of them have vitamins like vitamin E, omega 3's and 6's.

Almond or soy milk: Milk made from almonds or soybeans. They are safe for those who are lactose intolerant or have gluten and casein allergies. Almond milk is high in vitamins and low in calories. Almond and soy milk have as much calcium as cow's milk.

Aluminum free baking powder: We use this to make our baked foods rise without all the harmful effects of aluminum.

Agave nectar: Used instead of sugar and does not raise the sugar level in the body.

Organic cane sugar: Used in place of white sugar. Unrefined cane sugar contains seventeen amino acids, eleven minerals, and six vitamins, including antioxidants which are vitamin "SUPERHEROS" that fight the chemical "bad guys: that try to make you sick.

Sea Salt: Made from ocean water or water from saltwater lakes.

Flax oil: Oil from the flaxseed plant that is good for the heart, brain (concentration), healthy weight, and more.

DV = Daily Value: How much you should have for one day.

S.N.A.C. it up! Seasoning Packet: This healthy seasoning packet has organic spices that add flavor to your food using only the healthiest ingredients. It also saves you time and money. Ask your parents to buy the S.N.A.C. it up! seasoning packet, especially for those recipes where you want to do it yourself. Find out more on my website.

MEASURING

Measuring is VERY important when you are cooking. This is how we are able to make the same recipe over and over and over again and it tastes EXACTLY the same. If you GUESS, it can be a MESS, you will like it LESS, and…and...and….Just MEASURE so that it can be the BEST!!!

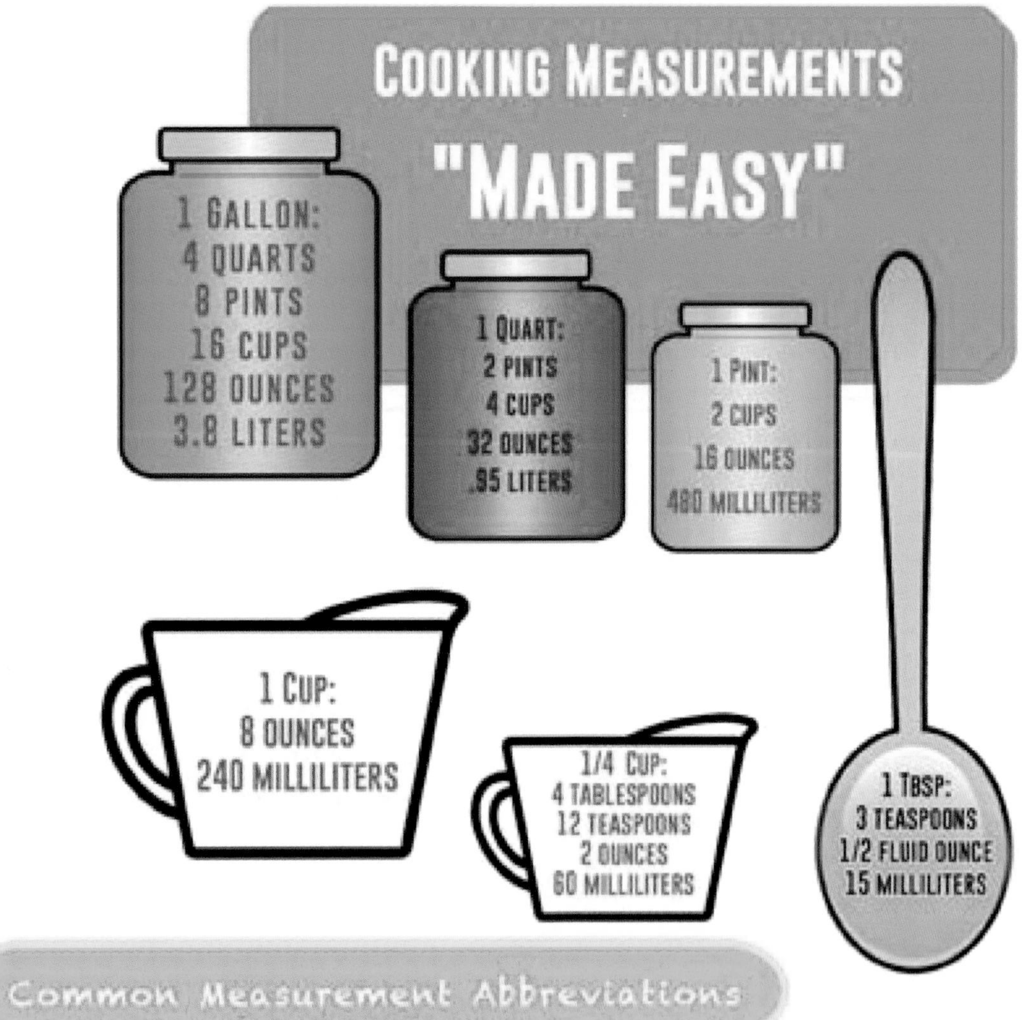

Common Measurement Abbreviations

tsp = teaspoon
tbsp = tablespoon
oz = ounce
c = cup
pt = pint
qt = quart
lb. = pound
opt = optional
oz = fluid ounces

DRINK LOTS OF WATER

(Half your body weight in ounces of water)

Before we get to the recipes, REMEMBER to ALWAYS have something raw before you eat your cooked food. My mom and dad always tell us to eat a big salad before our cooked vegetables, and fruit before our breakfast. My mom says that raw food is alive, and it helps to keep us alive. She always says, "Shi, eat your raw and have more energy." I eat my raw fruit and vegetables and I feel great every day. I love it! Ready for the recipes???????? Let's GO!!

BREAKFAST

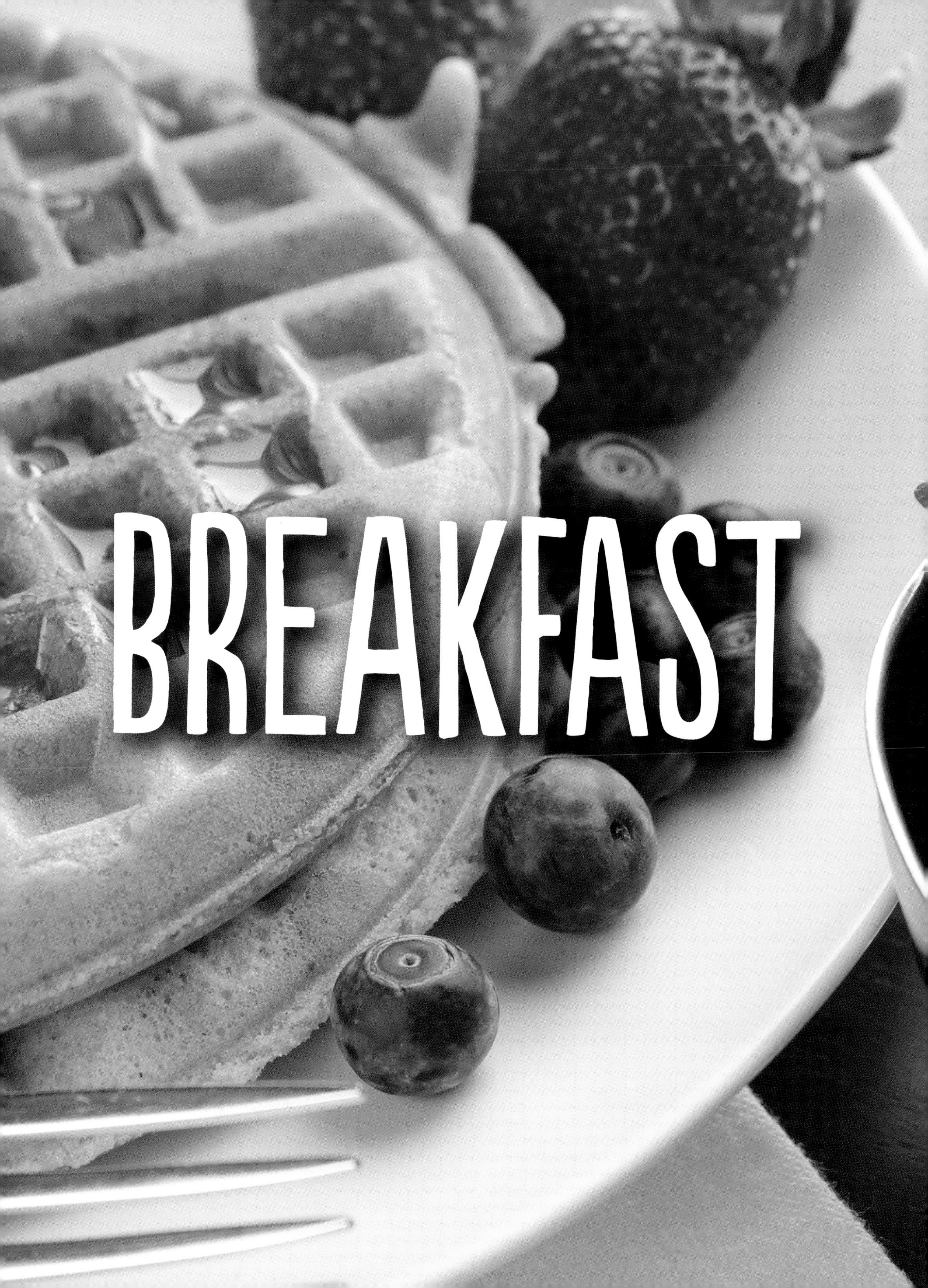

Granny's Cinnamon Apple Oatmeal

Prep Time: 10 minutes

We're gonna need:
1 cup quick oats
1 cup water
1 cup almond or soy milk
½ cup thinly sliced Granny Smith apples
1 tsp. cinnamon
1 tsp. earth balance butter spread
½ tsp. sea salt (optional)
1 tbsp. Pure Maple Syrup or Agave Nectar (especially if your sugar is high)

Lots of Love

Serving size: 1/2 of recipe
Servings in recipe: 2

Calories: 102
Potassium: 96mg
Sodium: 49mg
Sugars: 8g
Protein: 4g
Carbs: 13g
Fat: 1g
Vitamins: Vit C: 6% Vit A: 3% Calcium 14% Iron: 8%

1. Combine water, milk, oats, and salt in a small pot.
2. Place on the stove on low-medium heat for 5 minutes or until boiling. Stir constantly.
3. After 5 minutes, keep heat on low for another 5-10 minutes or until oats are thick enough.
4. Add apples, cinnamon, earth balance and maple or agave.
5. Place top on pot and turn stove off. Let sit for 2-3 minutes before serving.

Breakfast Hash Browns

Prep Time: 10 minutes
Completed Time: 20 minutes

We're gonna need:
1 cup Shredded potatoes
1/4 cup Tempeh bacon pieces
* **1/4 cup** chopped onion
* **2 tsp.** garlic powder
* **1 tbsp.** Tomato (optional)
* **1 tbsp.** red or green bell pepper (optional)
2 tbsp. Olive oil or other expeller pressed oil

Lots of love

Serving size: 1/2 of recipe
Servings in recipe: 2
Calories: 113
Calories from Fat: 11g
Potassium: 27mg
Carbs: 11g
Sodium: 65mg
Sugars: 3g
Protein: 2g
Vitamins: Vit C: 4% Vit A: 2% Calcium: 4% Iron: 4%

1. Pour oil in a pan and turn stove on medium heat.

2. After pan is hot, add all other ingredients.

3. Let potatoes brown before turning over.

4. After potatoes brown, get your taste buds ready, set, GO!

* Means that you can use the S.N.A.C. it up! Original Seasoning Packet instead of these ingredients.

Yummy Raw Granola Bars

Prep Time: 10 minutes
Completed Time: 20-30 minutes

We're gonna need:
1-3/4 cups rolled oats
1/2 cup mixed super food dried fruit (golden berries, mulberries, goji berries)
1/2 cup maple syrup, agave nectar or stevia (if your sugar is high)
1-1/2 tbsp pumpkin or chia seeds or almonds
A few dashes of cinnamon
1/4 cup room temperature creamy almond or peanut butter

Lots of Love

Serving Size: 1 bar
Calories: 191
Potassium: 32mg
Sodium: 36mg
Sugars: 17g
Protein: 16g
Carbs: 19g
Fat: 8g
Vitamins: Vit C: 43% Vit A: 95% Calcium: 11% Iron: 17%

1. Add all ingredients to a large mixing bowl.

2. Fold well until all the oats are soaked in nut butter and maple syrup.

3. Pour into a dish or cake pan. A good thickness for these bars is 3/4 of an inch.

4. Put in the fridge until just firm enough to slice, but still a little soft. Slice into 3-inch long squares and wrap in plastic wrap for on the go.

***Note:** The sugars in this recipe are naturally occurring and studies have shown that the berries in this study reduce blood sugar levels.

100% SATISFACTION GUARANTEED

FUN FACTS ABOUT OATS

- Oats were one of the earliest cereals cultivated by man. They were known in China thousands of years B.C.
- January is National "Oatmeal Month," and was created in the 1980's by The Quaker Oats Company's food service division because this is the month in which people buy more oatmeal than any other month of the year.
- Oatmeal is good for your heart. Approximately forty scientific studies show that eating oatmeal daily along with a low fat diet can reduce the risk of heart disease.
- Seventy-five percent of households in the United States have oatmeal in their pantry.
- Oatmeal cookies are the number one non-cereal usage for oats. Meatloaf is the second.
- An eighteen-ounce package of Old Fashioned Oats contains about 26,000 rolled oats. Tidbitfun.com

FUN FACTS ABOUT GOJI BERRIES

- Goji Berries are harvested by hand.
- The average goji vine produces berries for up to twenty years, however, after seven years the vine declines in production.
- The Goji Berry growing season is from June to October.
- Goji Berries are classified as a "Super Fruit" and many people say that super powers can cure almost any health problem.
- They have been used in China for over 6,000 years and are said to protect the liver, help eyesight, increase fertility, strengthen the legs, boost the immune system, improve circulation, and help you live a long time!
- Goji berries have the highest protein content of any fruit. Fruit that has protein???? Yes! 12% of Goji berries by weight are protein.
- Goji berries are high in vitamin A, B1, B2, B6, and vitamin E. They have more vitamin C by weight than any other food on earth. Wow!
- They have more iron than spinach.
- Goji berries have all 18 amino acids as well as 21 of the key trace minerals.

Breakfast Sausage Muffins

Prep Time: 10 minutes

We're gonna need:
1 cup unbleached flour or Bob's Red Mill Gluten-free Flour
1 teaspoon baking powder (aluminum free)
1 cup almond or soy milk
1 egg (egg replacer)
1 cup Daiya shredded cheddar cheese
1 tablespoon dried or fresh rosemary (optional)
3/4 - 1 cup Gimme Lean Sausage cooked and cut in pieces

Lots of Love

Serving size: 4 muffins
Calories: 208
Calories from Fat: 18g
Potassium: 357mg
Carbs: 24g
Sodium: 298mg
Sugars: 4.5g
Protein: 4g
Fat: 18g
Vitamins: Vit C: 4.9% Vit A: 10% Calcium: 10.6% Iron: 12.6%

1. Preheat the oven to 375 degrees. Grease a mini-muffin pan (holds 24 muffins). In a large bowl, whisk together the flour and baking powder; whisk in the milk and egg. Stir in the sausage and cheese and let stand for 10 minutes.

2. Stir and pour the batter into the mini-muffin cups with a spoon. Bake for 20-25 minutes, until golden.

3. Spread light layer of Earth Balance or Smart Balance (margarine) when ready to eat. Enjoy!

Almond or Peanut Butter Oatmeal Muffins

1 cup unbleached or wheat flour or Gluten free flour
2/3 cup Quick Cooking Oats
1/3 cup cocoa powder
3/4 cup evaporated cane sugar or 1/2 cup Agave Nectar
1 tbsp baking powder (aluminum free)
1/2 cup peanut or almond butter (creamy)
1/2 tsp salt
1 cup almond milk

Lots of Love

Serving size: 1 muffin

Calories: 199
Calories from fat: 7g
Potassium: 32mg
Carbs: 29g
Sodium: 149mg
Sugars: 16g
Protein: 8g
Vitamins: Vit A: 4% Vit D: 5% Vit E: 8%
Calcium: 12%
Iron: 12%

1. Preheat the oven to 350 degrees. Grease muffin pan with little cooking spray and set aside.

2. In a large bowl combine together the flour, oatmeal, cocoa powder, sugar, and baking powder.

3. In a small sauce pan, over low heat, melt peanut butter in milk, stirring constantly. Remove from heat and set aside to cool just a little.

4. Once the peanut or almond butter mixture is cool, mix it into the dry ingredients and stir well.

5. Spoon the batter into a muffin pan, filling it to the top of each cup.

6. Bake for 15 minutes or until a toothpick comes out clean. Enjoy!

FUN FACTS ABOUT ALMONDS

- Almonds were spread by humans in ancient times along the shores of the Mediterranean into northern Africa and southern Europe and more recently carried to other parts of the world, like California, in the United States.
- The almond tree is related to cherries, plums and peaches. There are sweet almonds and bitter almonds, and sweet almonds have varieties with soft and hard shells.
- The fruit of the almond is called a drupe, consisting of an outer hull and a hard shell with the seed or "nut" inside.
- Once almond trees start fruiting, they can produce almonds for more than 50 years.
- Almonds are good for the brain. Studies have shown that eating almonds in the morning helps growing children use their brains and helps their nerves.
- Almonds are good for the heart, cholesterol, bones, immune system, skin, inflammation, blood pressure, diabetes, weight loss, constipation, energy, and help to prevent Alzheimer's. (Organic Facts, 2013)

FUN FACTS ABOUT HONEYDEW MELON

- Honeydew melon has vitamin c and small amounts of other vitamins and minerals.
- It is low in fat.
- Honeydew melon is good for your nervous system, the heart, and muscles.
- It balances water in the body.
- It can be so sweet that you can eat it instead of sugary snacks.
- Honeydew melon is low in sodium.

Simple Summer Fruit Salad

Prep Time: 5 minutes

We're gonna need:
1 apple
1/2 orange for slicing
1/2 orange for squeezing
1/2 cup grapes
1/2 cup cantaloupe
or honeydew melon

Lots of Love

Serving size: 3/4 cup
Servings in recipe: 4
Calories: 41
Potassium: 3mg
Sodium: 7mg
Sugars: 17g
Protein: 2g
Carbs: 12g
Fat: 0g
Vitamins: Vit C: 91%
Vit A: 30% Calcium: 5%
Iron: 4%

1. Cut apple, 1/2 orange, cantaloupe, and honeydew melon into bite size pieces. Place in a big bowl.

2. Add grapes to the bowl of fruit. Stir ingredients.

3. Squeeze 1/2 orange over fruit.

4. Serve and enjoy. Put leftovers in the fridge. Yummy!

it

Monkey Pancakes

Prep Time: 5 minutes

We're gonna need:
1 cup unbleached flour or Bob's Red Mill Gluten-Free flour
1 tsp baking powder (aluminum free)
1/2 tsp baking soda (aluminum free)
1/2 tsp cinnamon (optional)
1 egg replacer
1/8 cup mashed banana
1 cup vanilla almond milk
3 tbsp coconut oil or any expeller pressed oil

Lots of Love

Serving size
1 medium size pancake

Calories: 265
Fat: 10.6g
Carbs: 27.45g
Protein: 5.14g
Sodium: 10mg
Potassium: 52mg
Calcium: 12%
Vitamins: Vit C: 8% Vit A: 1% Iron: 2% Sugars: .34g

1. Mix all dry ingredients (flour, baking powder, baking soda, and cinnamon).

2. Add milk, egg and melted oil. Stir for 1 minute.

3. Preheat pan and lightly grease the pan with coconut oil or any expeller pressed oil.

4. Pour about 1/2 cup of mix into the pan and wait until you see bubbles covering the top.

5. Turn your pancake over and let it cook on the other side until your spatula fits under the pancake without sticking.

6. When done, place your pancake on your plate and put your mashed bananas on top. You can eat with or without syrup!

FUN FACTS ABOUT BANANAS

- Bananas are a good source of dietary fiber.
- Bananas don't actually grow on trees. They grow on a giant herb.
- The phrase "going bananas" was first recorded in the Oxford English Dictionary because of the banana's connection with monkeys.
- They are a rich source of potassium, which helps keep your heart, nervous system and kidneys healthy.
- They have twice as much vitamin C as apples, pears, and grapes.
- They are a good source of vitamin B6. This vitamin is needed for the nervous system, for healthy skin and to produce energy in the body.
- Although they are very sweet, bananas have almost no fat.
- Bananas are one of the few foods to contain the 6 major vitamin groups.

LUNCH

Veggie Pocket Salad

Prep Time: 5 minutes

We're gonna need:
1 tbsp Daiya shredded Cheddar cheese
5 slices of cucumbers
1/4 cup Romaine lettuce
1 tsp Mustard
3 banana peppers
Olives (optional)
Pita bread cut in half

Lots of Love

Serving size: 1 pocket
Servings in recipe: 1

Calories: 184
Calories from Fat: 29
Potassium: 9mg
Carbs: 21g
Sodium: 271mg
Sugars: 9g
Protein: 7g
Fat: 1g
Vitamins: Vit C: 70%
Vit A: 27% Calcium: 12%
Iron: 19%

1. Fill pita with all ingredients.
2. Smile and enjoy!

FUN FACTS ABOUT BROWN RICE

- Brown rice is an ancient cereal that two-thirds of the world still live on.
- Brown rice gives you lots of energy and is used in the body for your brain, physical activity, your overall body and everyday growth and healing.
- Brown rice is packed with vitamins and other nutrients like potassium, protein, B vitamins, calcium, magnesium, iron, manganese, selenium, tryptophan, and more!
- Brown rice is low in fat and cholesterol free.
- Brown rice is also used for making straw, rope, paper, wine, crackers, cosmetics, packing material, and toothpaste.
- Compared with white rice, brown rice is more nutritious because it contains bran, which is a source of fiber, oils, B vitamins, and important minerals.

Garden Veggie Wrap

Prep Time: 10 minutes

We're gonna need:
4 Vegetarian chick'n Strips
1 tbsp cooked black beans
1 tbsp cooked corn or cooked brown rice
1 Whole wheat tortilla wrap
1/2 cup shredded romaine or green leaf lettuce
1 tbsp salsa

Lots of Love

Serving size: 1/2 wrap
Servings in recipe: 2

Calories: 47
Calories from Fat: 12
Potassium: 30mg
Carbs: 11g
Sodium: 150mg
Sugars: 1g
Protein: 7g
Fat: 0g
Vitamins: Vit C: 1%
Vit A: 15% Calcium: 8%
Iron: 8%

1. Place all ingredients on wrap, starting with lettuce, chick'n, black beans, corn and salsa.

2. Enjoy your healthy wrap!

Barbeque Crunch TLT

Prep Time: 10 minutes

We're gonna need:
2 slices of Tofurkey Tempeh Bacon
4 slices cucumber
tomato (optional)
onion (optional)
1 large piece romaine or green leaf lettuce
1 tbsp BBQ sauce
2 slices of bread

Lots of Love

Serving size: 1 sandwich
Servings in recipe: 1

Calories: 244
Potassium: 387mg
Sodium: 281mg
Sugars: 4g
Protein: 14g
Fat: 3g
Vitamins: Vit C: 23%
Vit A: 33% Calcium: 19%
Iron: 21% Carbs: 33g

1. Ask an adult to lightly grease a pan.
2. Place Tempeh Bacon in pan and cook on both sides until crisp.
3. Spread BBQ sauce on tempeh while in the pan. Turn on each side.
4. Place Tempeh on bread. Top with cucumbers, tomato, onion, and lettuce. Smile and enjoy!

Pocket Pie

Prep Time: 10 minutes
Completed Cook Time:
45 minutes

We're gonna need:
1/8 cup broccoli flower
1/8 cup frozen peas and carrot mix
Inside of 2 red potatoes
1/8 cup frozen Corn
***1 tsp.** onion powder
***1 tsp.** garlic powder
*1/4 tsp. Braggs Liquid Aminos or Sea Salt
1 tsp earth balance spread, depending on the size of the potato
2 ounces of water
Pita

Lots of Love

Serving size: 1/4 pocket pie
Servings in recipe: 4

Calories: 94
Calories from Fat: 25g
Potassium: 60mg
Carbs: 22g
Sodium: 300mg
Sugars: 2g
Protein: 13g
Fat: 0g
Vitamins: Vit C: 1%
Vit A: 30% Calcium: 16%
Iron: 16%

1. Bake a red potato.

2. In a small pot, boil water. Add all ingredients except the potatoes and earth balance spread. Cover and cook on low for 3-5 minutes.

3. Take out the inside of the potato and place it in a bowl.

4. Add all ingredients and stir, mixing well.

5. Place ingredients in a pita. Say thanks and enjoy.

* Means that you can use the S.N.A.C. it up! Original Seasoning Packet instead of these ingredients.

Chick'ny Not Chik'n Salad

Prep Time: 15 minutes
Completed Prep Time (after nuts are soaked):
20 minutes

We're gonna need:
1/2 cup almonds (soaked in water for 24 hours)
1/2 cup walnuts (soaked in water for 24 hours)
1/2 cup oat groats (soaked overnight in water)
*2 tsp onion powder
*2 tsp garlic powder
*1 tsp dried basil
*1 stalk of celery
1/2 carrot (cut in pieces)
1/4 red bell pepper
1 tbsp agave nectar or evaporated cane sugar
1 tbsp lemon juice
*1/2 tsp sea salt
1/2 tbsp water (if needed)

Lots of Love

Serving size: 1/4 cup
Servings in recipe: 8
Calories: 123
Calories from Fat: 70g
Potassium: 98mg
Carbs: 11g
Sodium: 301mg
Sugars: 4g
Protein: 5g
Fat: 2g
Vitamins: Vit C: 32%
Vit A: 38% Calcium: 11%
Iron: 10% Phosphorus: 122mg

This is a great recipe to take to school for lunch! I love this recipe. I make this with my mom, and it tastes soooo good. It also teaches me to be patient because it takes a long time for the nuts to soak.

1. Pour the water off of the soaked nuts and oat groats.
2. Place all ingredients, except lemon juice, in the food processor until smooth. If difficult to grind, add 1-2 tbsp water.
3. Squeeze lemon juice over it and stir.
4. Put on lettuce, bread, pita, or tortilla chips. Smile. Say thanks. Enjoy!!

*If you soak nuts overnight, it will double their nutritional value.

* Means that you can use the S.N.A.C. it up! Original Seasoning Packet instead of these ingredients.

Shi's Health Burger

Prep Time: 10 minutes
Completed Time:
20 minutes

We're gonna need:
1 cup cooked black beans or lentils
1/2 cup quick oats
1 flax egg
***1/2 tsp** vegetarian chicken style seasoning
***1 tbsp** chopped onions
***1 tbsp** garlic powder
*1 tsp basil
1 tbsp coconut, flax, olive, or expeller pressed safflower oil.
3/4 cup water
1 tbsp unbleached flour

Lots of Love

Serving size: 1 burger
Servings in recipe: 4-6
Calories: 168
Calories from Fat: 44
Potassium: 14mg
Sodium: 118mg
Sugars: 5g
Protein: 8g
Carbs: 12g
Fat: 5g
Vitamins: Vit C: 6%
Vit A: 1% Calcium 4%
Iron: 11%

1. Put oats, S.N.A.C. it up! original seasoning packet or chicken style seasoning, onions, garlic powder, basil, and water in a pot. Stir.

2. Turn stove on medium and cook until water is out.

3. Turn the stove off and add beans, flax egg, flour, and oil. Stir.

4. Put some flour on your hands and form into patties. Cook in a lightly oiled pan on the stove, allowing your burger to get a little crisp on each side. You can also bake these if you are not in a hurry.

5. Put burger on whole wheat bread and top with your favorite toppings. Smile. Give thanks. Aahhhh. Enjoy!

* Means that you can use the S.N.A.C. it up! Original Seasoning Packet instead of these ingredients.

FUN FACTS ABOUT WALNUTS

- Walnuts are said to have been around at least 4,000 years ago. Some say over 7,000.
- Walnuts are very healthy. They have the highest source of natural plant omega 3's called ALA. A 1/4 cup serving of walnuts gives 90% of the daily amount of omega 3's.
- Walnuts have magnesium, vitamin E, C, A, folate and other B vitamins.
- Eating walnuts is like wearing a seatbelt for your heart! (nutsforlife.com)
- Walnuts are shaped like the human brain and are actually VERY good for the brain. Some people call them the "Ultimate Brain Food."
- The modern walnut comes from the German "walnuss", meaning foreign nut.
- The walnut tree can grow up to 100 feet.

FUN FACTS ABOUT BEANS

- Beans are the large seeds of certain types of plants, and are technically a fruit.
- Beans are the only cultivated plants that actually add nutrients to its soil during the growing process rather than take away. Beans have nodules on their roots that add nitrogen to the soil instead of using it up.
- In ancient Rome, beans were thought to be so great that the four leading families took their names from them: Lentullus (lentil), Piso (pea), Cicero (chickpea), and Fabius (fava). (Crescent Dragonwagon, 2012)
- Bean carbohydrates have been proven to drastically improve the blood sugar levels in diabetics. Many adult-onset diabetics have been able to greatly reduce or stop taking their insulin through diets containing large amounts of beans. (Crescent Dragonwagon, 2012)
- In ancient Greece, minor public officials were elected by putting two different colored beans inside a "bean machine." Whoever picked the odd color bean got the job.
- Beans can be made into burgers, cakes, drinks, pies, fudge, muffins, jewelry, furniture (bean-bag chairs!), toys, and musical instruments. (oneseedchicago.com)

DINNER

Smiling Heart Pizza Muffins

Prep Time: 10 minutes
We're gonna need:
3/4 cup unbleached flour or Bob's Red Mill Gluten-free Flour
3/4 tsp baking powder (aluminum free)
3/4 cup almond or soy milk
1 egg (egg replacer)
1 cup Daiya shredded mozzarella cheese
1/2 cup pizza sauce
2 tbsp fresh or dried basil
1/2 cup vegetarian pepperoni (optional)
3/4 cup your favorite vegetable (broccoli, spinach, or mushroom)

Lots of love

Serving Size: 4 muffins
Calories: 114
Calories from fat: 18
Potassium: 51mg
Sodium: 280mg
Sugars: 5g
Protein: 5g
Carbs: 26g
Fat: 2g
Vitamins: Vit C: 9%
Vit A: 20% Calcium: 12%
Iron:3%

1. Preheat the oven to 375 degrees. Grease a mini-muffin pan (holds 24 muffins). In a large bowl, whisk together the flour and baking powder; whisk in the milk and egg. Stir in the pepperoni, cheese and vegetables; let stand for 10 minutes.

2. Stir and pour the batter into the mini-muffin cups with a spoon. Bake for 20-25 minutes, until golden.

3. Warm pizza sauce on the stove in a small pot. Stir in 2 tablespoons basil.

4. Dip the muffins in the pizza sauce. Enjoy!

*You can freeze the muffins in a freezer bag after cool. When ready to eat, place frozen muffins in preheated oven at 350 degrees for 8-10 minutes.

FUN FACTS ABOUT TOMATOES

- The tomato plant originated in South America and was domesticated by the Incas as early as 700 A.D. Back then, the tomato had many ruffles and ridges.
- Tomatoes are the richest source of lycopene, a carotenoid that scientists think could be important for the health of the prostate gland in men.
- The riper they are, the more lycopene they have.
- They are a good source of vitamin C (cherry tomatoes have even more vitamin C) and supply some vitamin E, folate and dietary fiber.
- Cherry tomatoes and those that are deep red in color are also a source of beta carotene.
- Studies have shown that people who eat large amounts of tomatoes or tomato products may be at lower risk of some kinds of cancer.
- Thomas Jefferson was known to love the tomato and tried to convince people it was a great fruit.
- Tomatoes are good for the heart. Studies have shown that people who eat tomatoes regularly are less likely to have a stroke.

Yummy Nachos

Prep Time: 20 minute

We're gonna need:
1 bag of tortilla chips
16 ounces of cooked pinto beans or 2 cans of organic pinto beans
1/2 package of Daiya Shredded Cheddar Cheese
1 cup ground TVP (Textured Vegetable Protein)
1/2 cup water
16 ounces Mild Taco Sauce
1 cup of Romaine lettuce

Lots of Love

Serving Size: 8 Chips with mild topping

Servings in recipe: 8-10

Calories: 191
Potassium: 32mg
Sodium: 36mg
Sugars: 17g
Protein: 16g
Carbs: 19g
Fat: 8g
Vitamins: Vit C: 43%
Vit A: 95% Calcium: 11%
Iron: 17%

1. Place beans and water in a pot. Turn stove on low for 5 minutes.

2. Add TVP. Cook for 5 minutes.

3. Add Taco sauce and cheese. Cook for 5-10 minutes on low until cheese melts.

4. Serve by placing chips on a plate and top with bean and cheese sauce. Top with lettuce.

Creamy "No Cook" Corn Soup

Prep Time: 10 minutes

We're gonna need:
3 cups corn fresh off the cob or frozen (non genetically modified)
2-1/2 cups water
1/2 cup raw cashews – soaked for at least an hour
1/4 sweet red pepper
***1 tsp** onion powder or 2 tsp fresh, cut onion
***1** small garlic clove or 1 tsp garlic powder
***2 tsp** Sea salt (optional)
3 tbsp olive or flax oil

Lots of love

Serving Size: 3/4 cup
Servings in recipe: 8
Calories: 215
Calories from Fat: 150
Potassium: 35mg
Sodium: 10mg
Sugars: 2g
Protein: 4g
Carbs: 21g
Fat: 4g
Vitamins: Vit C: 24%
Vit A: 5% Calcium: 2%
Iron: 4%

1. Combine 3 cups of corn with water, cashews, olive oil, garlic, and salt.

2. Place in blender and puree.

3. Pour soup into bowls. Place remaining corn on top.

* Means that you can use the S.N.A.C. it up! Original Seasoning Packet instead of these ingredients.

"Family Time" Pomegranate Vege Chicken

Prep Time: 20 minutes
We're gonna need:
4 pieces of thawed Gardein Vege Chicken Scallopini
2 tsp onion powder
2 tsp garlic powder
1 tsp basil
1/2 tsp paprika (optional)

For the glaze:
2 cups pomegranate juice
1 cup orange juice
1 tsp dried rosemary
3 garlic cloves
2-3 tbsp evaporated cane sugar or 2 tbsp of honey or agave nectar
Pinch of salt and pepper
2 tsp red wine vinegar

Lots of Love

Serving Size: 1 piece
Servings in recipe: 4
Calories: 106
Calories from Fat: 27g
Potassium: 51mg
Sodium: 149mg
Sugars: 5g
Protein: 6g
Carbs: 22g
Fat: 5g
Vitamins: Vit A: 10%
Calcium: 6% Iron: 8%

1. Make sure that your mom or dad is with you, and begin by speaking "love" thoughts.

2. Season Vege Chicken on both sides with onion powder, garlic powder, basil, and paprika.

3. Turn stove on medium, and lightly oil the pan.

4. Place chicken in pan and cook on both sides.

5. Prepare your pomegranate glaze by adding all ingredients in a small pot. Cook for about 15 minutes on high until thick.

6. Place your vege chicken on a plate and pour your delicious glaze over it.

7. Serve over brown rice with your favorite green vegetable. Yum, yum!

"This dish is meant to be made with your mom or dad. Have fun!

Spanish Mozzarella Sticks

Prep Time: 10 minutes

We're gonna need:
1/2 cup unbleached flour
1 tbsp Spanish paprika
2 flax eggs (2 tbsp golden flax meal + 4 tbsp water)
3 tbsp Almond, Ric or Soy Milk
***1 tbsp** dried Parsley Flakes
***1 tbsp** zesty seasoning (no salt)
***1 tbsp** basil
***1/2 tsp** sea salt
2 cups bread crumbs
1 block Daiya mozzarella or cheddar cheese

Lots of Love

Serving Size: 2 Cheese Sticks
Servings in recipe: 4
Calories: 22
Potassium: 12mg
Sodium: 290mg
Sugars: 2g
Protein: 4g
Carbs: 18g
Fat: 2g
Vitamins: Vit C: 43%
Vit A: 30% Vit E: 4%
Calcium: 6% Iron: 6%

1. In a bowl, place flour.
2. In another bowl, combine flax egg and milk.
3. In another bowl, combine bread crumbs and S.N.A.C. it up! seasoning pack or zesty, salt, basil, parsley, and paprika.
4. Cut cheese into 1/2 inch wide, long pieces. Dip cheese in flour, then flax mixture, and then bread crumbs.
5. Place in freezer for 15 minutes.
6. Heat oil in a pan until hot, and fry cheese sticks for 2-3 minutes.
7. Place cheese sticks on a plate with marinara sauce or nothing. Say "I love myself," eat, and enjoy!

* Means that you can use the S.N.A.C. it up! Original Seasoning Packet instead of these ingredients.

My Mom's Love Cornbread

Prep Time: 10 minutes
Completed Time: 45-55 minutes
We're gonna need:
2 cups organic yellow corn meal
3/4 cup unbleached flour or Bob's Red Mill Gluten Free flour
2 1/2 tsp aluminum free baking powder
1/4 cup evaporated cane sugar or 1/3 cup agave nectar
1 tsp sea salt
2-1/2 cup almond, rice, or coconut milk
1/8 cup organic, virgin coconut oil
1 flax egg

Lots of Love

Serving Size: 1 2x2 piece
Servings in recipe: 10
Calories: 142
Calories from fat: 18
Potassium: 48mg
Sodium: 101mg
Sugars: 2g
Protein: 8g
Carbs: 28g
Fat: 10g
Vitamins: Vit C: 43% Vit A: 4% Calcium: 16% Iron: 13% Vit E: 13% Vit D: 7% Phosphorus: 33mg

1. Preheat oven to 375 degrees
2. Combine all dry ingredients. Add agave nectar with liquid ingredients
3. Add milk, agave nectar (if you're using it), oil, and flax egg.
4. Stir for 1-2 minutes
5. Grease a nine-inch pan with oil
6. Pour cornbread mixture in pan and put in oven for 35-45 minutes or until golden brown

Cornbread Taco Pie

Prep Time: 20 minutes
Completed Time: 1 hour

We're gonna need:
1-1/2 cups dry ground TVP (Textured Vegetable Protein)
1 taco seasoning pack
1 eight-ounce can tomato sauce
1-1/2 cups water
3 cups cornbread mix (already mixed in a bowl)
1/2 cup broccoli
1/2 cup spinach
4 tbsp Tofutti Better than Sour cream
1/2 pack Daiya shredded cheddar cheese

Lots of Love

Serving Size: 1 3x3 piece

Servings in recipe: 8-10
Calories: 125
Calories from fat: 30
Potassium: 475mg
Sodium: 283mg
Sugars: 2g
Protein: 14g
Carbs: 18g
Fat: 4g
Vitamins: Vit C: 13%
Vit A: 22% Calcium: 12%
Iron: 18%

1. Preheat oven to 375 degrees
2. Boil water and then add TVP. Let cook for 5-10 minutes
3. Add taco seasoning pack to TVP and stir.
4. Add tomato sauce and stir.
5. Add broccoli, spinach, and sour cream to the sauce and stir.
6. Spread 1-1/2 cups cornbread mix in bottom of a glass pan
7. Spread all of your sauce mixture on top of the layer of cornbread mix in the pan.
8. Spread the other 1-1/2 cups of cornbread mix on top
9. Add lots of love
10. Place in the oven for 40 minutes or until cornbread top is golden brown.

Raw Kale/Collard Salad

Prep Time: 5 minutes

We're gonna need:
1 cup organic collards (thinly sliced)
1/4 cup organic Kale greens (thinly sliced)
1/4 cup fresh shredded carrots
1/8 cup shredded purple cabbage
***1 tbsp** onion powder
***1 tbsp** garlic powder
1/8 cup organic roasted red pepper salad dressing
1/8 cup organic French tomato salad dressing

Lots of Love

Serving size: 1/2 cup
Servings in recipe: 4

Calories: 33
Calories from Fat: 14
Potassium: 22mg
Carbs: 6g
Sodium: 182mg
Sugars: 1g
Protein: 2g
Vitamins: Vit C: 7%
Vit A: 48% Vit K: 34%
Calcium: 11% Iron:3%

1. Place sliced kale and collard greens in a big bowl. Mix.

2. Add all of the other ingredients. Stir

3. Make sure that you smile as you stir, and think about how happy your body is going to be when you eat this.

4. Put a top on your bowl and put it in the refrigerator for one hour or more. My mom and I let it sit overnight unless we are really hungry.

5. Put it on a plate or in a bowl, put on your biggest smile and Enjoy!!!

* Means that you can use the S.N.A.C. it up! Original Seasoning Packet instead of these ingredients.

FUN FACTS ABOUT COCONUT

- Coconut water is a universal blood donor and is identical to human blood plasma. It is called the "fluid of life." Coconut water was used as an IV drip in World War II. This means that it went straight into the bloodstream! (consciouscoconuts.com).
- Coconut oil is good for digestion, food allergies, cancer, heart, people that get really tired, skin, and hair. (earthclinic.com).
- Coconut oil is a good fat and helps people lose weight.
- Coconut oil can help with blood sugar and thyroid, while helping our bodies fight viruses and bacteria that can cause illness.
- Coconut shells are used for art, decoration, crafts, cups, bowls, pots for plants, lamps, and many more items that you use everyday!

FUN FACTS ABOUT KALE GREENS

"Is there anything fun about greens?"

- Kale is mainly grown in East and West Africa, Middle and Western Europe, and North America.
- Kale has a large amount of Vitamin K, Vitamin C and Vitamin A, and manganese. It also has good amounts of folate, phosphorous, calcium, potassium, Omega 3s, protein, iron, magnesium, Vitamin B1, Vitamin B2, Vitamin B3, and Vitamin E. Kale also has forty-five different phytonutrients.
- Kale is said to prevent cancer.
- Kale is a part of the brassica family along with cabbage, cauliflower, and broccoli.
- This leafy vegetable can protect the body from some deadly and dangerous diseases.
- Kale is good for eyes, digestive system, skin, cells, brain, and the immune system.

I sure hope that you will start eating kale with me. I love it!

Quesadilla

Prep Time: 5 minutes
Completed Time:
15 minutes

We're gonna need:
1 cup cooked Black beans
1/2 cup Daiya shredded cheddar cheese
1/2 cup romaine or green eaf lettuce
1/4 cup shredded green or purple cabbage (cooked or uncooked)
8 whole wheat flour tortillas
Salsa (to taste)

Lots of Love

Serving size: 2 Quesadillas
Servings in recipe: 8
Calories: 145
Calories from Fat: 20g
Potassium: 119mg
Carbs: 19g
Sodium: 269mg
Sugars: 1g
Protein: 7g
Fat: 0g
Vitamins: Vit C: 4%
Vit A: 3% Calcium: 1%
Iron: 1%

1. Place 1 tortilla in the bottom of a pan.
2. Spread 1/2 of all ingredients on the tortilla in the pan.
3. Cover with 1 tortilla to make a pie. Place the top on the pan.
4. Cook on low-medium heat for 3-5 minutes or until brown at the bottom.
5. Turn over and cook for another 3-5 minutes or until brown.
6. Cut in fourths, dip in salsa, smile and enjoy!

Sweet and Sour Sauce

Prep Time: 8-10 minutes

We're gonna need:
1 tbsp ice water
1 tbsp cornstarch (non gmo)
3/4 cup of pineapple juice
1/4 cup Bragg's Apple Cider Vinegar
1 tbsp evaporated cane sugar
1 tbsp Tomato paste or ketchup
1 tsp salt

Lots of Love

Serving size: 1 tbsp

Calories: 6
Calories from Fat: 0g
Potassium: 17mg
Carbs: 6g
Sodium: 68mg
Sugars: 2g
Protein: 0g
Fat: 0g
Vitamins: Vit C: 5%
Vit A: 1% Calcium: 1%
Iron: 1%

1. In a small bowl, mix ice water and corn-starch and mix until fully dissolved. Set aside.
2. Place pineapple juice in a small saucepan.
3. Add vinegar, sugar and salt to pan and heat on medium high, stirring with a whisk.
4. Once simmering, drizzle in cornstarch mixture and whisk quickly until sauce thickens. Remove from heat and pour sauce into a bowl.
5. Serve immediately with sweet and sour vegetable pasta.

Sweet and Sour Vegetable Pasta

Prep Time: 5-10 minutes
Completed Prep Time: 25 minutes

We're gonna need:
2 cups cooked whole grain Angel hair pasta
1 cup fresh Broccoli flowers
1/2 cup cauliflower (optional)
1/4 cup sliced carrots
1/4 cup thinly sliced green or purple cabbage
***1 tbsp** fresh onion or 2 tbsp onion powder
***1** garlic clove or 1 tbsp garlic powder
3 tbsp Natural Sweet and Sour Sauce

Lots of Love

Servings in recipe: 6
Calories: 231
Calories from Fat: 0g
Potassium: 30mg
Carbs: 25g
Sodium: 100mg
Sugars: 4g
Protein: 12g
Fat: 0g
Vitamins: Vit C: 59%
Vit A: 100% Calcium: 6%
Iron: 5%

Nutritional Facts are for are for 1 serving

1. Steam broccoli, cauliflower, carrots, and cabbage until done. Be sure not to over-cook because they will become mushy.
2. Place steamed veggies in a pan and add all other ingredients. Stir really well.
3. Cook on low heat for about two minutes.
4. Put sweet and sour veggies on top of the angel hair pasta. Smile and enjoy! Oh!!! Don't forget the love!

* Means that you can use the S.N.A.C. it up! Original Seasoning Packet instead of these ingredients.

Crazy 8 Pasta

Prep Time: 20 minutes
Completed Prep Time:
45 minutes

We're gonna need:
1/2 cup Broccoli
1 cup spinach
1/2 cup cooked kidney beans
1/2 cup (TVP) Texturized Vegetable Protein
1/2 cup water
1/2 package whole grain Rotini pasta
1 jar organic Garden Vegetable or Tomato Basil Spaghetti Sauce
1 tbsp agave nectar or evaporated cane sugar
***1 tbsp** Sea Salt
***3 tbsp** garlic powder
***3 tbsp** onion powder

Lots of Love

Servings in recipe: 6
Calories: 81
Calories from Fat: 2g
Potassium: 317mg
Carbs: 31g
Sodium: 290mg
Sugars: 9g
Protein: 11g
Fat: 2g
Vitamins: Vit C: 30%
Vit A: 22% Calcium: 11%
Iron: 19%

Nutritional Facts are for 1/2 cup pasta with 1/2 cup vegetables

1. Cook pasta according to the directions on the package.
2. In another pot, add water and 2 S.N.A.C. it up! ORIGINAL seasoning packets or salt, garlic powder, and onion powder. Turn your stove on low-medium.
3. As soon as water begins to boil, add TVP and stir for 10-15 seconds. Add kidney beans, spinach, and broccoli. Cover pot and cook for 3-5 minutes on low heat.
4. Add spaghetti sauce to vegetables and simmer for 5 minutes.
5. Serve vegetables over pasta and enjoy!

DESSERT

Vanilla Ice Cream

Prep Time: 15 minutes
Completed Time:
1 hour

We're gonna need:
1 package Tofutti Cream Cheese
1 cup Almond Breeze Vanilla Almond Milk
3/4 cup evaporated cane sugar
1 cup Non-dairy French Creamer
1 tsp vanilla extract
1 Firm or Extra Firm Silken Tofu

Lots of Love

1. Place all ingredients in the blender and blend until smooth.
2. Pour into an ice cream maker and let it mix for 25 minutes.
3. Pour into frozen bowl from ice cream maker. Let it stay in freezer for about 45 min. to an hour.
4. Take out and eat. Try not to eat the whole thing!

Butter Pecan Ice Cream

Prep Time: 15 minutes
Completed Time:
1 hour

We're gonna need:
1 package Tofutti Cream Cheese
1 cup Almond Breeze Vanilla Almond Milk
3/4 cup evaporated cane sugar
1 cup Non-dairy French Creamer
1 tsp vanilla extract
1 Firm or Extra Firm Silken Tofu
2 tbsp Earth balance
1/2 cup pecans or walnuts

Lots of Love

1. Place all ingredients in the blender and blend until smooth.
2. Pour into an ice cream maker and let it mix for 20 minutes.
3. Add nuts while ice cream maker is still on. Let it mix for another 5 minutes.
4. Pour into frozen bowl from ice cream maker. Let it stay in freezer for about 45 min. to an hour.
5. Take out and eat. Smile and enjoy!

Summer Whipped Fruit Pie

Prep Time: 10 minutes
Completed Time:
30 minutes

We're gonna need:
1/4 cup red grapes
1/4 cup ripe cantaloupe
1/4 cup honeydew melon
1 package of Tofutti non dairy cream cheese
1/8 cup evaporated cane sugar
2 tbsp of almond, soy, or coconut milk
1 tsp vanilla extract
Graham Cracker crust (optional)

Lots of Love

1. Slice cantaloupe and honeydew melon into bite size pieces, and mix with grapes in a bowl.
2. In a separate bowl, put non dairy cream cheese, sugar, milk, and vanilla extract. Mix with a whisk or a hand blender for 1 minute.
3. Place fruit in pie dish with or without graham cracker crust.
4. Spread whipped topping on top of the fruit until it's evenly spread.
5. Refrigerate for 30-45 minutes to help it set. This is best if kept in the fridge or freezer until ready to eat.
6. Think good thoughts, smile, and enjoy!

No Bake Healthy Brownies

Prep Time: 15 minutes
Completed Time: 45 minutes

We're gonna need:
1-1/2 cup walnuts
1-1/2 cup pecans
1 cup dates (remove pits)
2/3 cup cacao nibs
3 tbsp agave nectar
4-6 tbsp shredded unsweetened coconut (optional)
1/2 tsp vanilla extract
Pinch of sea salt

Lots of Love

1. Place walnuts and pecans in food processor and process until finely chopped.

2. Add cacao and then dates, agave nectar (optional), coconut (optional), vanilla and salt. Press the pulse button slowly, and then process until it is smooth and well blended.

3. Place in an 8-inch square or round pan. If using a regular pan, line it with parchment paper, allowing the paper to drape over the sides.

4. Refrigerate for 30 minutes or so to help it set. This is best if kept in the fridge or freezer until ready to eat.

Makes approximately twenty-four - 1" brownies

Honeydew Lemon Cupcakes

Prep Time: 10 minutes
Completed Time: 30 minutes

We're gonna need:
1 cup almond or soy milk
1 teaspoon apple cider vinegar
1-1/2 cups flour
1/2 tsp baking powder
3/4 tsp baking soda
1/4 tsp salt
1/4 cup expeller pressed safflower oil
2/3 cup evaporated cane sugar
1 tsp vanilla extract
1/4 cup fresh squeezed lemon juice
1 tbsp lemon zest

Lots of Love

Icing:
3/4 cup organic powdered sugar or 1/2 cup agave nectar
Eight-ounces soy cream cheese softened
1 tbsp lemon juice
1/4 cup juiced honeydew melon

Blend all ingredients with a hand mixer and spread on your cupcakes. Yum!

1. Preheat oven to 350 degrees. Line a muffin pan with muffin liners. Spray liners with oil.

2. In a small bowl, stir together milk and apple cider vinegar. Let sit for 5 minutes.

3. In a large bowl, combine flour, baking powder, baking soda and salt.

4. In a separate large bowl, combine milk, oil, sugar, vanilla, lemon juice and zest.

5. Add dry ingredients to wet and stir until well combined.

6. Pour batter into lined muffin tins until each is 3/4 full.

7. Bake 20-22 minutes or until you can stick a toothpick in the center and it comes out clean. Let cool completely before frosting. Don't forget to add "love" before serving.

Marshmallow Ice Cream Cake

Prep Time: 25 minutes
Completed Time:
2-1/2 hours

We're gonna need:
1 cup graham cracker crumbs
3 tbsp melted earth balance or smart balance butter
1 tbsp cinnamon
2 quarts vanilla almond or soy ice cream OR homemade ice cream from this cookbook
1-2 cups vegan marshmallows broken in small pieces

Lots of Love

1. Stir the graham cracker crumbs, earth (smart) balance, cinnamon, and love in a bowl until even. Press this mixture with your hands into the bottom of a 9-inch round pan. Set in freezer for 10-15 minutes.

2. Spread the vanilla ice cream over the crust evenly. Place in the freezer for 2 hours. Smile.

3. Take the cake from the freezer and top with the marshmallows. Put in the freezer for 15 more minutes. Eat and enjoy!

*To make graham cracker crumbs, ask an adult to take 8 graham crackers and grind them in a grinder or blender.

SNACK

Frozen Strawberry Raspberry Yogurt Pops

Prep Time: 5 minutes
Completed Time:
1 to 2 hours

We're gonna need:
1 6-oz. container of soy vanilla or coconut flavored yogurt
1 large strawberry or 2 small ones without the leaf
5 raspberries
1 tbsp of milk (almond, soy or coconut)

We're gonna need:
small paper cups
wooden popsicle sticks
(available in craft stores)
plastic wrap

Lots of Love

Calories: 57
Calories from Fat: 12g
Potassium: 11mg
Carbs: 29g
Sodium: 5mg
Sugars: 6g
Protein: 11g
Fat: 0g
Vitamins: Vit C: 9%
Vit A: 1% Calcium: 13%
Iron: 3%

1. Place all ingredients in the blender. Blend for 1 minute.

2. Pour mixture into paper cups. Fill them almost to the top.

3. Stretch a small piece of plastic wrap across the top of each paper cup.

4. Using the popsicle stick, poke a hole in the plastic wrap. Stand the stick straight up in the center of the cup.

5. Put the cups in the freezer until the mixture is frozen solid.

6. Remove the plastic wrap and carefully peel away the paper cup. Enjoy your healthy pop!!!

Sassy Applesauce

Prep Time: 10 minutes

We're gonna need:
2 small red apples
2 tbsp lemon juice
2 tsp agave nectar or evaporated cane juice or sugar granules
2 pinches of cinnamon (optional)

We're gonna need:
knife (you'll need help from your mom or dad)
blender or food processor
measuring spoons
serving bowls

Lots of Love

1. Peel the apples and cut them into small pieces. Throw out the core.

2. Put the apple pieces and lemon juice into the blender or food processor. Blend until the mixture is very smooth.

3. Pour the mixture into a bowl and stir in the sugar and cinnamon.

Calories: 80
Calories from Fat: 0g
Dietary Fiber: 6g
Potassium: 5mg
Carbs: 22g
Sodium: 1mg
Sugars: 18g
Protein: 11g
Fat: 0g
Vitamins: Vit C: 25%
Vit A: 2% Calcium: 1%
Iron: 2%

FUN FACTS ABOUT STRAWBERRIES

- Each strawberry has about 200 seeds on it.
- They are not really berries. They are in the rose family.
- Strawberries are very high in vitamin C and potassium.
- The ancient Romans thought that strawberries could cure bad breath and chronic fainting.
- There is a museum in Belgium just for strawberries.
- They make muscles and the brain work better.

FUN FACTS ABOUT APPLES

- Apples are nutritious, giving you natural energy, carbohydrates, vitamin c, potassium, boron, vitamin E, iron, calcium and vitamin A when eaten raw.
- The skin of the apple is good for hair growth.
- Peeling the apple takes away 90-95% of the nutrients.
- A man named John Chapman, born in 1774, began a one-man mission to have apple trees growing everywhere. Stories about Mr. Chapman say that he walked from Massachusetts to Illinois with a bag of apple seeds, showing people how to grow them. Other stories say that he planted apple trees hoping to sell them to settlers for six cents per tree. He became known as **Johnny Appleseed**.
- Apples float in water because they are 25% air.
- They are high in fiber, good for your colon.
- An apple per day may just keep the doctor away. Try it!

FUN FACTS ABOUT CARROTS

- Doctors say that carrots improve eye sight, especially night vision.
- They are high in vitamin A and beta carotene.
- Good source of fiber.
- In the 1500's, Dutch carrot growers invented the orange carrot in honor of the House of Orange, the Dutch Royal Family. They crossbred pale yellow carrots with red carrots.
- The longest carrot ever recorded was nearly 17 feet long.
- The largest carrot ever recorded weighed 18.985 pounds.

Cucarrot Salad

Prep Time: 5 minutes

We're gonna need:
2 Whole Cucumbers
1 Shredded Carrot
1/8 cup your favorite salad dressing
Multi-colored Tortilla strips (optional)

Lots of Love

Serving size: 3/4 cup
Servings in recipe: 4

Calories: 28
Calories from Fat: 1g
Potassium: 0mg
Carbs: 6g
Sodium: 73mg
Sugars: 4g
Protein: 0g
Fat: 0g
Vitamins: Vit C: 9%
Vit A: 54% Calcium: 4%
Iron: 4%

1. Slice cucumbers keeping as much of the peel as you can. Most of the vitamins are in the peel.

2. Mix the shredded carrots and sliced cucumbers in a bowl. Pour salad dressing and stir.

3. Top with the tortilla strips and enjoy!! This is great to take in your lunch box.

Carob Joy-Nut Bars

Prep Time: 15 minutes

We're gonna need:
2 cups Carob Chips
1/4 cup coconut flakes **(optional)**
1/4 cup almonds or any nut you like
3 tbsp almond butter
2 tsp flax oil
water (for boiling only)

Lots of Love

Serving size: 1 bar
Servings in recipe: 6

Calories: 342
Calories from Fat: 92g
Potassium: 27mg
Carbs: 2g
Sodium: 0mg
Sugars: 0g
Protein: 5g
Fat: 10g
Vitamins: Vit C: 0%
Vit A: 0% Calcium: 2%
Iron: 2%

1. Place water in a pan until it reaches 1-2 inches high. Turn on medium heat until the water boils.
2. Turn the stove off
3. In a separate small pot, place carob chips.
4. Place the pot with the carob chips inside of the pot on the stove.
5. Stir carob chips until completely melted.
6. Add all other ingredients one at a time. Mix well after each ingredient.
7. Pour into a 9-inch square glass dish and smooth with a spoon.
8. Put in the fridge just long enough to get a little hard.
9. Lick the spoon for your tasting and so that you can tell your mom and dad that you didn't waste any food.
10. After your bars are ready, ask your mom or dad to help you cut them with a knife 3 inches long.

Apple Peanut Butter Cup

Prep Time: 5 minutes

We're gonna need:
1 apple sliced
3-4 tsp peanut or almond butter
1 tbsp carob chips

Lots of Love

Servings in recipe: 1

Calories: 185
Calories from Fat: 108g
Potassium: 68mg
Carbs: 24g
Sodium: 85mg
Sugars: 9g
Protein: 1g
Fat: 4g
Vitamins: Vit C: 10%
Vit A: 54% Calcium: 13%
Iron: 8%

1. Place sliced apples on a small plate.
2. Drizzle almond or peanut butter over the apples
3. Sprinkle carob chips over apples
4. Enjoy every bite and smile!

Shi-Trail mix

Prep Time: 5 minutes

We're gonna need:
1/2 cup raw cashews
1/4 cup raisins
1/4 cup raw sunflower seeds
1/8 cup sesame sticks

Lots of Love

Servings in recipe: 4

Calories: 180
Calories from Fat: 115g
Potassium: 68mg
Carbs: 19g
Sodium: 3mg
Sugars: 6g
Protein: 7g
Fat: 7g
Vitamins: Vit C: 1%
Vit A: 1% Calcium: 5%
Iron: 10%

1. Put all ingredients in a bowl and mix.

2. Pour into a small snack bag. Enjoy and share with your best friend.

DRINKS

Apple Zinger Juice

Prep Time: 5 minutes

We're gonna need:
2 organic apples
1 organic carrot
1/4 inch ginger
1/4 lemon without the peel

Lots of Love

Serving Size: 1/2 cup
Servings in recipe: 2
Calories: 99
Calories from Fat: 0g
Potassium: 198mg
Carbs: 21g
Sodium: 20mg
Sugars: 18g
Protein: 1g
Fat: 0g
Vitamins: Vit C: 24%
Vit A: 137% Calcium: 2%
Iron: 3%

Always, ALWAYS have an adult with you when juicing. The different parts of a juicer can be REALLY sharp.

1. Cut all of the ingredients small enough to fit in the opening of your juicer.
2. Place a cup under the spout
3. Place all ingredients in juicer
4. Smile and say "thanks" as you watch the juice come out (This is one of the most important steps).
5. Enjoy and feel your body saying "thank you."

FUN FACTS ABOUT GINGER

- Ginger is good for a stomach ache.
- It has healthy oils, protein, calcium iron, manganese, folic acid, choline, phosphorus, vitamin c, silicon, vitamin B3, inositol, and more....
- You only have to use a LITTLE bit when juicing in order to get all of the vitamins. Children should not use a lot when juicing.
- It has been said to have more nutrients than most people have ever heard of.
- Ginger has been used a lot for the cold, flu, cough, and sore throat.
- Some people use it as a natural breath freshener.
- Ginger helps control heart rate and blood pressure.

Ginger Lemonade

Prep Time: 5 minutes
Prep time if boiling ginger: 20 minutes

We're gonna need:
2-3 inch piece of Ginger cut in pieces or juiced and put aside
3 lemons squeezed
6 cups of water
3/4-1 cup agave nectar or fresh stevia herb to taste

Lots of Love

Calories: 40
Calories from Fat: 0g
Potassium: 0mg
Carbs: 4g
Sodium: 2mg
Sugars: 4g
Protein: 1g
Fat: 0g
Vitamins: Vit C: 0%
Vit A: 0% Calcium: 0%
Iron: 1%

Always, ALWAYS have an adult with you when juicing. The different parts of a juicer can be REALLY sharp.

1. Boil pieces of ginger on low for 15 minutes or use juiced ginger.
2. Strain the water from the ginger and put in a pitcher or mix water with juiced ginger.
3. Squeeze lemons into the ginger water.
4. Add agave nectar or stevia herb. If using stevia herb, let sit in hot ginger water or boil 2 of the 6 cups of water and add 10-12 tsp stevia herb. Turn off the stove. Let sit for 10 min. Strain the herbs and add this water to the "juiced" ginger water.
5. Drink warm or place in the fridge for a cool, healthy drink for later.

My mom says that ginger is good for everything. We make this ginger lemonade when someone is sick or well. It's soooo good that I can't stop drinking it. I can hear my mom saying, "It's good for your stomach, heart, sugar level, and much more!"

The nutritional facts in this recipe do not include agave nectar and stevia herb. The two sweeteners are very different. In studies, real stevia herb has been shown to lower blood sugar. Real stevia herb is green.

Enjoy your ginger lemonade!

Healthy Sugar Juice

Prep Time: 5 minutes

We're gonna need:
1/2 cucumber
1 large green apple or 2 small ones
1 stalk of celery

Lots of Love

Serving Size: 1
Calories: 101
Calories from Fat: 1g
Potassium: 230mg
Carbs: 27g
Sodium: 35mg
Sugars: 17g
Protein: 1g
Fat: 0g
Vitamins: Vit C: 12%
Vit A: 8% Calcium: 1%
Iron: 6%

Always, ALWAYS have an adult with you when juicing. The different parts of a juicer can be REALLY sharp.

1. Cut all of the ingredients small enough to fit in the opening of your juicer.
2. Place a cup under the spout
3. Place all ingredients in juicer
4. Smile and say "thanks" as you watch the juice come out (This is one of the most important steps).
5. Enjoy and feel your body saying "thank you."

Gotta Have My Greens Juice?

Prep Time: 5 minutes

We're gonna need:
2 apples
1/2 cup spinach

Lots of Love

Calories: 144
Calories from Fat: 5g
Potassium: 296mg
Carbs: 38g
Sodium: 11mg
Sugars: 26g
Protein: 2g
Fat: 0g
Vitamins: Vit C: 23%
Vit A: 19% Calcium: 4%
Iron: 5%

Always, ALWAYS have an adult with you when juicing. The different parts of a juicer can be REALLY sharp.

1. Cut all of the ingredients small enough to fit in the opening of your juicer.

2. Place a cup under the spout

3. Place all ingredients in juicer

4. Smile and say "thanks" as you watch the juice come out (This is one of the most important steps).

5. Enjoy and feel your body saying "thank you."

A FEW THOUGHTS TO CHANGE YOUR THOUGHTS

In order to be healthy, you have to have healthy thoughts. It can be soooooo fun learning to be more positive. Watch how much better you feel about yourself and others when you start speaking and believing great things. I haven't always felt good about myself, and I began to tell myself some of the same things that I am sharing with you. I didn't believe these sayings at first, but in a short time I began to believe ALL of them. Now, I LOVE it, LIVE it, and see impossible things happening just because I changed my thoughts. Have fun!

Love,

Shi

Positive Thoughts Puzzle

Directions: Find the positive sayings and then repeat them **everyday** and see what happens!

```
L I A M T H A N K F U L I R I K Y
U I S E N D L O V E X A T L B D V
F Y I E H M Z J F G M R O K O H M
R L F Z V H G Y N S A V L B O A Y
E D E A M O O P A M E U Y X K G B
D N E J I Z L F S E F M G U E J O
N E L I V M E O X I F I C A W W D
O I C H O O S E T O B E H A P P Y
W R A Y L M R U E Y Y R G G L T I
M F L W A C A R G Y S W V V M X S
A M M I I E A D Z Y W A F W B P P
I A G S B C I G K V W F E D Z Q E
I I I M E L U F R E W O P M A I R
L N A K I C P F Q I O O K F A U F
G I A I L O V E M Y S E L F M I E
U T G N I H T Y N A O D N A C I C
I Y H T L A E H T A E I J K O A T
```

1. I love myself
2. My body is perfect
3. I am wonderful
4. I send love
5. I am so smart
6. I eat healthy
7. I am easy to love
8. I am friendly
9. I am beautiful
10. I choose to be happy
11. I am safe
12. I am thankful
13. I feel calm
14. I take care of my body
15. I love exercising
16. I am powerful
17. I can do anything

S.H.A.R.E.W.I.T.H. Puzzle

Directions: Find all of the words that will help you to *SHAREWITH.*

```
I E T T Z D C Q F O O E V H T
L N R E T S W R S B S J U P S
O I U L O S U Z H I O G M L K
V H S L Z I E E C L T E Z E C
E S T B T J O R H H Q O X H A
M N S A I C E P E E L S W I J
Y U A D N X B E O J S H W T G
S S S S E N L U F K N A H T N
E W D E P D Z W D N Z B F R I
L R A C E K B B A L Q A H U P
F E R R H E D B X T U K H H M
S I L E S E L B A T E G E V U
A Y M T O U T S I D E R U U J
D R E S H E A L T H Y F O O D
E T P C P H D L R U T N Y S Y
```

1. Sunshine
2. Healthy food
3. Air
4. Rest
5. Exercise
6. Water
7. I love myself
8. Trust
9. Thankfulness
10. Help
11. Jumping jacks
12. Outside
13. Vegetables
14. Fruit
15. Sleep
16. Tell bad secrets
17. Hug the elderly

What's My New Favorite Food?

Directions: Find the healthy foods in the puzzle and eat them as much as you can.

```
B A G A V E N E C T A R X T B
L T H W L G B R O C C O L I S
A I G C W A A Y A K E D M E E
C U F I Q B P L Y Z V J I C C
K R K N V B P M S E A R I A Z
B F V A W A L B M D R R R T A
E E S G L C E E F E N R G L G
A P P R S E S T B W O O M V G
N A I O F L G W O T G O M I G
S R N V R P A R S M N Q N L R
U G A Y O R B H E D A G L Y A
V Y C F T U M V M E E T D D O
N S H S Y P W I O R N B O Q Q
Y U S T U N L A W X V S U E E
C H H G M K M C O C O N U T S
```

1. Broccoli
2. Spinach
3. Carrots
4. Kale greens
5. Tomatoes
6. Walnuts
7. Almonds
8. Purple cabbage
9. Black beans
10. Brown rice
11. Almond milk
12. Agave nectar
13. Apples
14. Grapefruit
15. Strawberries
16. Organic
17. Ginger
18. Coconuts

Do I REALLY Love Myself?

Directions: Find how many times the PHRASE "I Love Myself" appears in this puzzle.

```
T H F I L O V E M Y S E L F U
F L E S Y M E V O L I I F L H
N F Q S Z G F O T E O L L E N
F I L E S Z L G Q W O O E S G
Q X I E V F E O P S L V S Y O
H K J L S C S Z E G E E Y M J
H E W V O Y Y U Y A N M M E A
U J D I J V M P L D H Y E V W
X N C M G C E E Q C T S V O L
Q B P Z W J V M V V T E O L E
H Z Q E K T O F Y O B L L I Y
C Q J A Y V L U Y S L F I F H
W N I I J U I X U A E I X D E
I L O V E M Y S E L F L J J E
O K Y P U B T U M F R N F Q X
```

In this puzzle, the Phrase "I Love Myself" appears _____ times.

Do you love yourself as many times as this puzzle tells you to say it?

THANK YOU

I would like to thank God for giving me this opportunity to teach children how to be healthy. I would like to thank my mom and dad for supporting me, and believing in my talents. I thank my brothers, Miykal and Amari for always saying "Do good Shi," and helping me anytime I ask. I'd like to thank my brother, Miykal, who owns AwesomeEditz video company. He is the BEST editor and cameraman (teenager, lol), and makes so many of S.N.A.C it up! videos come alive.

My grandma, Mary Beard "Mommy," granddad, Joe Beard "Big Daddy," Grandma Thelma Holland, Uncle David Curry who tasted my food when other people thought that I was too young to cook delicious food, Aunties Jeannette, Alisa and Toot for always supporting me, Aunty Lorie, uncles Duane, Brotha (Christopher Beard), and Jerome, Ti Ti Angela Thompson for ALWAYS being there for S.N.A.C. it up! when it was just you and my parents, Uncle David & Aunty Marian Lewis (Living Water Productions) who pray with me, film me, and have been a part of my team from before the beginning, Mr. Eric (Thompson) who came up with the original name (SNACK) and believed in me, Godmommy (Sonia Dean) and my God family, Uncle Ryan & Samantha Marshall, my sis, Melany Brown, Nathaniel & Simone Bronner, Christine Gayle, Billy Floyd, "G" Mom (Flora Brown) for believing in me and supporting me with a BIG smile, Yvette Lewis Gates, AC Mclean (ACM PR), Ella Mathews, Pastor S. Jack, Celebrity Chef "J" Shawain Whyte who has supported me soooooo much, taught me so many culinary skills and become my family, D Healthstore, Recharda Grayden (Coca Cola), Chef Byron Green for all of your support and phenomenal training, Christopher McBrown (Neptune Studios), Maranatha SDA church, Boulevard SDA church, and the Spirit Reign Communications and Publishing Family.

Special thanks to my S.N.A.C. it up! team that meets EVERY week to make sure that my dreams stay alive: Angela Thompson (Chief Administrative Officer, Off Camera motivator, Personal Assistant and more!, Patricia Campbell (Creative Director), Nicole Harris (Communications Coordinator), Christine Gayle (Curriculum Advisor and Board Member), Jonathan Curry (Music Director and CIO), and Celeste Curry, COO.

PRODUCTS COMING IN 2016-2017

S.N.A.C. it up! DVD and DVD Curriculum 2016
S.N.A.C. it up! Affirmation Videos and CD's 2016
S.N.A.C. it up! T-Shirts
S.N.A.C. it up! Aprons
S.N.A.C. it up! Multivitamin
S.N.A.C. it up! Super Kid's Positive Thoughts Activities Workbook
Workshops NOW!

"Shi" Presents The

Subscription

We invite you to give the special child in your life the experience of a wholesome and healthy activity that will last him/her a lifetime.

Your child will experience cooking with "Shi" once a month, as well as a live question and answer session after the cooking class. He/she will receive a monthly newsletter filled with cooking tips, activities, affirmations and more! An email will be sent out one week before the cooking class giving instructions on the ingredients and utensils needed for the upcoming class.

This subscription is not just for your child. Parents will also receive helpful tips on how to raise a healthy child in a fast food society, as well as special affirmations just for you from Celeste Curry - Shi's mom, a family counselor of eighteen years.

For only $4.99 per month, you will give a child the life changing skills of healthy cooking, eating AND thinking!

To purchase subscriptions or for more information, go to: www.snacitup.com and click on the subscription tab in the top menu.

To become a S.N.A.C. it up! member and receive news and updates on Shi and S.N.A.C. it up! go to snacitup.com I would love to hear from you!

KEEP IN TOUCH!

To find out more about "Shi" and S.N.A.C. it up!, play exciting games, and become a member, please go to my website **snacitup.com.**
I would LOVE to hear from you!

NOTES

NOTES